TO: _____

FROM: _____

DATE: _____

WORD POWER
SERIES
for
HEALING

A Parallel Healing Prayer Book
of scriptures from the King James Version and the
Amplified Bible for receiving your healing
based upon the power of The Word of God and faith!

KEVIN E. KEMP, SR.

WORD POWER SERIES FOR HEALING

Published & Edited by:
Yanér Publishing, PKMI, Inc.
Editor-in-Chief, Pamela R. Kemp
P.O. Box 35751
Fayetteville, NC 28303
Office:919.455.6930

Published for Author:
Apostle Kevin E. Kemp, Sr.
International Healing Evangelist
Kevin Kemp Ministries (KKM) International Inc.
Attn: Kevin Kemp Media Ministries
P.O. Box 35751
Fayetteville, North Carolina 28303
Office: 919.455.6930

ISBN-10: 0692273042
ISBN-13: 978-0-692-27304-3

DEDICATION

MOST SPECIAL THANKS TO MY BEST FRIEND AND LIFE AND KINGDOM MINISTRY PARTNER MY LOVING WIFE, PAMELA

I dedicate this first WORD POWER SERIES book to my most special and loving wife, best friend, and life-long Kingdom ministry partner, Pamela! You are the most valued person on this earth that my good God has given me. Thank you for all the many sacrifices you have made for us and for inspiring me to continue the family and ministry vision for our lives. You are the BEST! ∎

ACKNOWLEDGEMENTS

I would like to thank and honor my children Kevin Jr. and Kevina (BG), Terrell and Pierre, and especially honor my mother, BAMI-FOC National Mother, Mother M.D. Kemp, for all of her years of prayer and support in my ministry call. Thank you Mom!

Special thanks to my spiritual son and daughter, Deacon Marvin and Deaconess Katrina Mack, and their four fun children (our grand-kids): Devin, Catherine, Korin, and Evin, for all of your hard work and service in helping Lady Pamela and I to fulfill our purpose and destiny assignments. We love you dearly!

Special appreciation to my (FOFOCI) Pastor and Chief Apostle, Bishop Kyle C. Searcy, for your leadership, support, book writing advise, and encouragement; and, to my (AFCIFOCM) Prophet and Bishop, Dr. Antonio Burroughs for your kingdom-building covenant and ministry partnership in "Confronting the Culture and Defending the Faith!" I appreciate both of your friendships and ministry accountability. ∎

CONTENTS

Introduction   9

Prepare to be Healed   11

1. Old Testament Healing Scriptures   12

2. New Testament Healing Scriptures   33

3. The Warfarecology of Healing   77
   Author's Commentary on
   Ephesisian 6:12

4. The Will of God *for* You   83
   Author's Commentary on
   3 John 1-4

5. Ingredients *for* Healing &   87
   Manifestation (The Incubation Period)

6. Prayer Decree *for* You (Family or Friend)   90

7. Book Reading Thoughts,   93
   Revelations, and Testimonies

8. Testimonies & KKM Faith   98
   Partnership Contact Information

INTRODUCTION

As I travel around the world in the International Healing Ministry, I see many, many healings, miracles, signs, and wonders from the healing virtue of our Lord Jesus Christ. Because of these healings and miracles, tens of thousands of people world-wide have come to the saving knowledge that Jesus Christ is truly the Son of God. They believe that He died on the cross of calvary for the sins of the world, and that He rose again from the dead. He is ALIVE and is seated at the right hand of Father God continuing to make intercession for us.

I believe the main reasons we see so many healings and miracles in our world-wide crusades and conferences is so the unbelievers might believe: 1) the truth of the Gospel of Jesus Christ; 2) the truth which is written in the scriptures of the Holy Bible; 3) the truth that Jesus is alive; 4) the truth that He is the Healer; and, 5) the truth that He is the Messiah and Son of God!

I believe the primary way born-again believers are healed is through belief, faith, and their confession of the power of the Word of God as written in the Holy Bible. As Christians experience battles of sickness and disease, we must activate and decree the Word of God against all forces and forms of darkness, death, sickness, and disease that will try to disable our ability to prosper and be in good health, even as our soul prospers.

My endeavor in writing this book is to make it easier for those who are believing God for their healing and miracle but are shut-in at home, in hospitals, nursing homes, etc. to study, confess, decree, and meditate on healing scriptures directly from the Word of God with ease.

This book is not designed to replace your Bible. It is a quick and ready resource to use to pray for yourself and others who may need to be reminded of the victory over sickness and disease that we already have in the finished work of our Lord and Savior, Jesus Christ.

What's really special about this WORD POWER SERIES book is the parallell-healing scriptures from the King James Version and the Amplified (AMP) bibles. The translations are together for better understanding, revelation and declaration. I pray it will be a help and immediate blessing to every reader and hearer who receives, and believes!

It's also a great gift for anyone in need of healing and a miracle! I recommend every bible student, healing evangelist, pastor, ministry leader, intercessor or believer who prays for the sick to use this resource for scripture memorization and as a quick reference and access to healing scriptures and prayer with and for people. ∎

PREPARE TO BE HEALED!

General Confession and Prayer

Lord Jesus Christ, I believe that You are the Son of God, the Messiah who came in the flesh to destroy the works of the devil. I believe that by Your stripes I was healed, that You died on the cross for my sins, and that You rose again from the dead. I choose now to give You my life.

I now confess all my sins and repent (*turn from the devil's influence in my life, and turn now to the Holy Spirit's influence over my life*). I claim Your forgiveness and cleansing from all unrighteousness and sin that I have ever committed in my life. I believe that Your blood cleanses me now from all my sins. Thank you Lord for redeeming me, cleansing me, saving me, justifying me, and sanctifying me by Your blood.

Thank you Lord for saving me. I now receive all the benefits of my salvation in Jesus' Name. Amen! ∎

Chapter

OLD TESTAMENT HEALING SCRIPTURES

EXODUS
Exodus 12:23

23 For the LORD will pass through to smite the Egyptians; and when he seeth the blood upon the lintel, and on the two side posts, the LORD will pass over the door, and will not suffer the destroyer to come in unto your houses to smite *you.*

AMP

23 *For the Lord will pass through to slay the Egyptians; and when He sees the blood upon the lintel and the two side posts, the Lord will pass over the door and will not allow the destroyer to come into your houses to slay you.*

Exodus 15:26

26 And said, If thou wilt diligently hearken to the voice of the LORD thy God, and wilt do that which is right in his sight, and wilt give ear to his commandments, and keep all his statutes, I will put none of these diseases upon thee, which I have brought upon the Egyptians: for I *am* the LORD that healeth thee.

AMP

26 *Saying, If you will diligently hearken to the voice of the Lord your God and will do what is right in His sight, and will listen to and obey His commandments and keep all His statues, I will put none of the diseases upon you which I brought upon the Egyptians, for I am the Lord Who Heals you.*

Exodus 23:25

25 And ye shall serve the LORD your God, and he shall bless thy bread, and thy water; and I will take sickness away from the midst of thee.

AMP

25 *You shall serve the Lord your God; He shall bless your bread and water, and I will take sickness from your midst.*

NUMBERS
Numbers 21:8-9

8 And the LORD said unto Moses, Make thee a fiery serpent, and set it upon a pole: and it shall come to pass, that every one that is bitten, when he looketh upon it, shall live.

9 And Moses made a serpent of brass, and put it upon a pole, and it came to pass, that if a serpent had bitten any man, when he beheld the serpent of brass, he lived.

AMP

8 *And the Lord said to Moses, Make a fiery serpent [of bronze] and set it on a pole; and everyone who is bitten, when he looks at it, shall live.*

9 *And Moses made a serpent of bronze and put it on a pole, and if a serpent had bitten any man, when he looked to the serpent of bronze [attentively, expectantly, with a steady and absorbing gaze], he lived.*

2 KINGS
2 Kings 20:1-7

1   In those days was Hezekiah sick unto death. And the prophet Isaiah the son of Amoz came to him, and said unto him, Thus saith the LORD, Set thine house in order; for thou shalt die, and not live.

2   Then he turned his face to the wall, and prayed unto the LORD, saying,

3   I beseech thee, O LORD, remember now how I have walked before thee in truth and with a perfect heart, and have done *that which is* good in thy sight. And Hezekiah wept sore.

4   And it came to pass, afore Isaiah was gone out into the middle court, that the word of the LORD came to him, saying,

5   Turn again, and tell Hezekiah the captain of my people, Thus saith the LORD, the God of David thy father, I have heard thy prayer, I have seen thy tears: behold, I will heal thee: on the third day thou shalt go up unto the house of the LORD.

6   And I will add unto thy days fifteen years; and I will deliver thee and this city out of the hand of the king of Assyria; and I will defend this city for mine own sake, and for my servant David's sake.

7   And Isaiah said, Take a lump of figs. And they took and laid *it* on the boil, and he recovered.

AMP

1   *In those days Hezekiah became deadly ill. The prophet Isaiah son of Amoz came and said to him, Thus says the Lord: Set your house in order, for you shall die; you shall not recover.*

²   Then Hezekiah turned his face to the wall and prayed to the Lord, saying,

³   I beseech You, O Lord, [earnestly] remember now how I have walked before You in faithfulness and truth and with a whole heart [entirely devoted to You] and have done what is good in Your sight. And Hezekiah wept bitterly.

⁴   Before Isaiah had gone out of the middle court, the word of the Lord came to him:

⁵   Turn back and tell Hezekiah, the leader of My people, Thus says the Lord, the God of David your [forefather]: I have heard your prayer, I have seen your tears; behold, I will heal you. On the third day you shall go up to the house of the Lord.

⁶   will add to your life fifteen years and deliver you and this city [Jerusalem] out of the hand of the king of Assyria; and I will defend this city for My own sake and for My servant David's sake.

⁷   And Isaiah said, Bring a cake of figs. Let them lay it on the burning inflammation, that he may recover.

2 CHRONICLES
2 Chronicles 20:3 & 15

³   And Jehoshaphat feared, and set himself to seek the LORD, and proclaimed a fast throughout all Judah.

¹⁵   And he said, Hearken ye, all Judah, and ye inhabitants of Jerusalem, and thou king Jehoshaphat, Thus saith the LORD unto you, Be not afraid nor dismayed by reason of this great multitude; for the battle is not yours, but God's.

3   *Then Jehoshaphat feared, and set himself [determinedly, as his vital need] to seek the Lord; he proclaimed a fast in all Judah.*

15   *He said, Hearken, all Judah, you inhabitants of Jerusalem, and you King Jehoshaphat. The Lord says this to you: Be not afraid or dismayed at this great multitude; for the battle is not yours, but God's.*

NEHEMIAH
Nehemiah 8:10-12

10   Then he said unto them, Go your way, eat the fat, and drink the sweet, and send portions unto them for whom nothing is prepared: for *this* day *is* holy unto our Lord: neither be ye sorry; for the joy of the LORD is your strength.

11   So the Levites stilled all the people, saying, Hold your peace, for the day *is* holy; neither be ye grieved.

12   And all the people went their way to eat, and to drink, and to send portions, and to make great mirth, because they had understood the words that were declared unto them.

AMP

10   *Then [Ezra] told them, Go your way, eat the fat, drink the sweet drink, and send portions to him for whom nothing is prepared; for this day is holy to our Lord. And be not grieved and depressed, for the joy of the Lord is your strength and stronghold.*

11   *So the Levites quieted all the people, saying, Be still, for the day is holy. And do not be grieved and sad.*

¹² *And all the people went their way to eat, drink, send portions, and make great rejoicing, for they had understood the words that were declared to them.*

JOB
Job 42:10

¹⁰ And the LORD turned the captivity of Job, when he prayed for his friends: also the LORD gave Job twice as much as he had before.

AMP

¹⁰ *And the Lord turned the captivity of Job and restored his fortunes, when he prayed for his friends; also the Lord gave Job twice as much as he had before.*

PSALMS
Psalm 6:2-4

² Have mercy upon me, O LORD; for I *am* weak: O LORD, heal me; for my bones are vexed.

³ My soul is also sore vexed: but thou, O LORD, how long?

⁴ Return, O LORD, deliver my soul: oh save me for thy mercies' sake.

AMP

² *Have mercy on me and be gracious to me, O Lord, for I am weak (faint and withered away); O Lord, heal me, for my bones are troubled.*

³ *My [inner] self [as well as my body] is also exceedingly disturbed and troubled. But You, O Lord, how long [until You return and speak peace to me]?*

4   *Return [to my relief], O Lord, deliver my life; save me for the sake of Your steadfast love and mercy.*

Psalm 23:1-3

1   The LORD *is* my shepherd; I shall not want.

2   He maketh me to lie down in green pastures: he leadeth me beside the still waters.

3   He restoreth my soul: he leadeth me in the paths of righteousness for his name's sake.

AMP

1   *The Lord is my Shepherd [to feed, guide, and shield me], I shall not lack.*

2   *He makes me lie down in [fresh, tender] green pastures; He leads me beside the still and restful waters.*

3   *He refreshes and restores my life (my self); He leads me in the paths of righteousness [uprightness and right standing with Him—not for my earning it, but] for His name's sake.*

Psalm 25:17-18

17   The troubles of my heart are enlarged: *O* bring thou me out of my distresses.

18   Look upon mine affliction and my pain; and forgive all my sins.

AMP

17   *The troubles of my heart are multiplied; bring me out of my distresses.*

18   *Behold my affliction and my pain and forgive all my sins [of thinking and doing].*

Psalm 30:2

2   O LORD my God, I cried unto thee, and thou hast healed me.

AMP

2   *O Lord my God, I cried to You and You have healed me.*

Psalm 34:19

19   Many *are* the afflictions of the righteous: but the LORD delivereth him out of them all.

AMP

19   *Many evils confront the [consistently] righteous, but the Lord delivers him out of them all.*

Psalm 61:5-6

5   For thou, O God, hast heard my vows: thou hast given *me* the heritage of those that fear thy name.

6   Thou wilt prolong the king's life: *and* his years as many generations.

AMP

5   *For You, O God, have heard my vows; You have given me the heritage of those who fear, revere, and honor Your name.*

6   *May You prolong the [true] King's life [adding days upon days], and may His years be to the last generation [of this world and the generations of the world to come].*

Psalm 91:1-4, 16

1   He that dwelleth in the secret place of the most High shall abide under the shadow of the Almighty.

2   I will say of the LORD, *He is* my refuge and my fortress: my God; in him will I trust.

3   Surely he shall deliver thee from the snare of the fowler, *and* from the noisome pestilence.

4   He shall cover thee with his feathers, and under his wings shalt thou trust: his truth *shall be thy* shield and buckler.

16   With long life will I satisfy him, and shew him my salvation.

AMP

1   *He who dwells in the secret place of the Most High shall remain stable and fixed under the shadow of the Almighty [Whose power no foe can withstand].*

2   *I will say of the Lord, He is my Refuge and my Fortress, my God; on Him I lean and rely, and in Him I [confidently] trust!*

3   *For [then] He will deliver you from the snare of the fowler and from the deadly pestilence.*

4   *[Then] He will cover you with His pinions, and under His wings shall you trust and find refuge; His truth and His faithfulness are a shield and a buckler.*

16   *With long life will I satisfy him and show him My salvation.*

Psalm 92:14

14   They shall still bring forth fruit in old age; they shall be fat and flourishing;

AMP

14   [Growing in grace] they shall still bring forth fruit in old age; they shall be full of sap [of spiritual vitality] and [rich in the] verdure [of trust, love, and contentment].

Psalm 103:1-5

1   (A Psalm of David.) Bless the LORD, O my soul: and all that is within me, bless his holy name.

2   Bless the LORD, O my soul, and forget not all his benefits:

3   Who forgiveth all thine iniquities; who healeth all thy diseases;

4   Who redeemeth thy life from destruction; who crowneth thee with lovingkindness and tender mercies;

5   Who satisfieth thy mouth with good things; so that thy youth is renewed like the eagle's.

AMP

1   [A Psalm] of David. Bless (affectionately, gratefully praise) the Lord, O my soul; and all that is [deepest] within me, bless His holy name!

2   Bless (affectionately, gratefully praise) the Lord, O my soul, and forget not [one of] all His benefits—

3   Who forgives [every one of] all your iniquities, Who heals [each one of] all your diseases,

4 *Who redeems your life from the pit and corruption, Who beautifies, dignifies, and crowns you with loving-kindness and tender mercy;*
5 *Who satisfies your mouth [your necessity and desire at your personal age and situation] with good so that your youth, renewed, is like the eagle's [strong, overcoming, soaring]!*

Psalm 105:37

37 He brought them forth also with silver and gold: and *there was* not one feeble *person* among their tribes.

AMP

37 *He brought [Israel] forth also with silver and gold, and there was not one feeble person among their tribes.*

Psalm 107:19-20

19 Then they cry unto the LORD in their trouble, *and* he saveth them out of their distresses.
20 He sent his word, and healed them, and delivered *them* from their destructions.

AMP

19 *Then they cry to the Lord in their trouble, and He delivers them out of their distresses.*
20 *He sends forth His word and heals them and rescues them from the pit and destruction.*

Psalm 118:17-18

17 I shall not die, but live, and declare the works of the LORD.

---

18   The LORD hath chastened me sore: but he hath not given me over unto death.

AMP
17   *I shall not die but live, and shall declare the works and recount the illustrious acts of the Lord.*

18   *The Lord has chastened me sorely, but He has not given me over to death.*

Psalm 147:3
3   He healeth the broken in heart, and bindeth up their wounds.

AMP
3   *He heals the brokenhearted and binds up their wounds [curing their pains and their sorrows].*

PROVERBS
Proverbs 3:7-8
7   Be not wise in thine own eyes: fear the LORD, and depart from evil.

8   It shall be health to thy navel, and marrow to thy bones.

AMP
7   *Be not wise in your own eyes; reverently fear and worship the Lord and turn [entirely] away from evil.*

8   *It shall be health to your nerves and sinews, and marrow and moistening to your bones.*

Proverbs 4:20-22

20   My son, attend to my words; incline thine ear unto my sayings.

21   Let them not depart from thine eyes; keep them in the midst of thine heart.

22   For they *are* life unto those that find them, and health to all their flesh.

AMP

20   *My son, attend to my words; consent and submit to my sayings.*

21   *Let them not depart from your sight; keep them in the center of your heart.*

22   *For they are life to those who find them, healing and health to all their flesh.*

Proverbs 17:22

22   A merry heart doeth good *like* a medicine: but a broken spirit drieth the bones.

AMP

22   *A happy heart is good medicine and a cheerful mind works healing, but a broken spirit dries up the bones.*

Proverbs 16:24

24   Pleasant words are as an honeycomb, sweet to the soul, and health to the bones.

AMP

24   *Pleasant words are as a honeycomb, sweet to the mind and healing to the body.*

Proverbs 18:21

21   Death and life are in the power of the tongue: and they that love it shall eat the fruit thereof.

AMP

21   *Death and life are in the power of the tongue, and they who indulge in it shall eat the fruit of it [for death or life].*

<u>ISAIAH</u>
Isaiah 10:27

27   And it shall come to pass in that day, *that* his burden shall be taken away from off thy shoulder, and his yoke from off thy neck, and the yoke shall be destroyed because of the anointing.

AMP

27   *And it shall be in that day that the burden of [the Assyrian] shall depart from your shoulders, and his yoke from your neck. The yoke shall be destroyed because of fatness [which prevents it from going around your neck].*

Isaiah 35:3-6

3   Strengthen ye the weak hands, and confirm the feeble knees.

4   Say to them *that are* of a fearful heart, Be strong, fear not: behold, your God will come *with* vengeance, *even* God *with* a recompence; he will come and save you.

5   Then the eyes of the blind shall be opened, and the ears of the deaf shall be unstopped.

6   Then shall the lame *man* leap as an hart, and the tongue of the dumb sing: for in the

wilderness shall waters break out, and streams in the desert.

AMP

3   *Strengthen the weak hands and make firm the feeble and tottering knees.*

4   *Say to those who are of a fearful and hasty heart, Be strong, fear not! Behold, your God will come with vengeance; with the recompense of God He will come and save you.*

5   *Then the eyes of the blind shall be opened, and the ears of the deaf shall be unstopped.*

6   *Then shall the lame man leap like a hart, and the tongue of the dumb shall sing for joy. For waters shall break forth in the wilderness and streams in the desert.*

Isaiah 40:29-31

29   He giveth power to the faint; and to *them that have* no might he increaseth strength.

30   Even the youths shall faint and be weary, and the young men shall utterly fall:

31   But they that wait upon the LORD shall renew *their* strength; they shall mount up with wings as eagles; they shall run, and not be weary; *and* they shall walk, and not faint.

AMP

29   *He gives power to the faint and weary, and to him who has no might He increases strength [causing it to multiply and making it to abound].*

30   *Even youths shall faint and be weary, and [selected] young men shall feebly stumble and fall exhausted;*

31   *But those who wait for the Lord [who expect, look for, and hope in Him] shall change and renew their strength and power; they shall lift their wings and mount up [close to God] as eagles [mount up to the sun]; they shall run and not be weary, they shall walk and not faint or become tired.*

Isaiah 53:4-5

4   Surely he hath borne our griefs, and carried our sorrows: yet we did esteem him stricken, smitten of God, and afflicted.

5   But he *was* wounded for our transgressions, *he was* bruised for our iniquities: the chastisement of our peace *was* upon him; and with his stripes we are healed.

AMP

4   *Surely He has borne our griefs (sicknesses, weaknesses, and distresses) and carried our sorrows and pains [of punishment], yet we [ignorantly] considered Him stricken, smitten, and afflicted by God [as if with leprosy].*

5   *But He was wounded for our transgressions, He was bruised for our guilt and iniquities; the chastisement [needful to obtain] peace and well-being for us was upon Him, and with the stripes [that wounded] Him we are healed and made whole.*

Isaiah 58:6-11

6   *Is* not this the fast that I have chosen? to loose the bands of wickedness, to undo the heavy burdens, and to let the oppressed go free, and that ye break every yoke?

7 *Is it* not to deal thy bread to the hungry, and that thou bring the poor that are cast out to thy house? when thou seest the naked, that thou cover him; and that thou hide not thyself from thine own flesh?

8 Then shall thy light break forth as the morning, and thine health shall spring forth speedily: and thy righteousness shall go before thee; the glory of the LORD shall be thy rearward.

9 Then shalt thou call, and the LORD shall answer; thou shalt cry, and he shall say, Here I *am*. If thou take away from the midst of thee the yoke, the putting forth of the finger, and speaking vanity;

10 And *if* thou draw out thy soul to the hungry, and satisfy the afflicted soul; then shall thy light rise in obscurity, and thy darkness *be* as the noonday:

11 And the LORD shall guide thee continually, and satisfy thy soul in drought, and make fat thy bones: and thou shalt be like a watered garden, and like a spring of water, whose waters fail not.

AMP

6 *[Rather] is not this the fast that I have chosen: to loose the bonds of wickedness, to undo the bands of the yoke, to let the oppressed go free, and that you break every [enslaving] yoke?*

7 *Is it not to divide your bread with the hungry and bring the homeless poor into your house—when you see the naked, that you cover him, and that you hide not yourself from [the needs of] your own flesh and blood?*

8 *Then shall your light break forth like the morning, and your healing (your restoration and*

the power of a new life) shall spring forth speedily; your righteousness (your rightness, your justice, and your right relationship with God) shall go before you [conducting you to peace and prosperity], and the glory of the Lord shall be your rear guard.

9 Then you shall call, and the Lord will answer; you shall cry, and He will say, Here I am. If you take away from your midst yokes of oppression [wherever you find them], the finger pointed in scorn [toward the oppressed or the godly], and every form of false, harsh, unjust, and wicked speaking,

10 And if you pour out that with which you sustain your own life for the hungry and satisfy the need of the afflicted, then shall your light rise in darkness, and your obscurity and gloom become like the noonday.

11 And the Lord shall guide you continually and satisfy you in drought and in dry places and make strong your bones. And you shall be like a watered garden and like a spring of water whose waters fail not.

JEREMIAH
Jeremiah 17:14

14 Heal me, O LORD, and I shall be healed; save me, and I shall be saved: for thou *art* my praise.

AMP

14 Heal me, O Lord, and I shall be healed; save me, and I shall be saved, for You are my praise.

Jeremiah 30:17

17a For I will restore health unto thee, and I will heal thee of thy wounds, saith the Lord.

AMP

17a *For I will restore health unto thee, and I will heal thee of thy wounds, says the Lord.*

EZEKIEL
Ezekiel 37:3-6

3 And he said unto me, Son of man, can these bones live? And I answered, O Lord GOD, thou knowest.

4 Again he said unto me, Prophesy upon these bones, and say unto them, O ye dry bones, hear the word of the LORD.

5 Thus saith the Lord GOD unto these bones; Behold, I will cause breath to enter into you, and ye shall live:

6 And I will lay sinews upon you, and will bring up flesh upon you, and cover you with skin, and put breath in you, and ye shall live; and ye shall know that I *am* the LORD.

AMP

3 *And He said to me, Son of man, can these bones live? And I answered, O Lord God, You know!*

4 *Again He said to me, Prophesy to these bones and say to them, O you dry bones, hear the word of the Lord.*

5 *Thus says the Lord God to these bones: Behold, I will cause breath and spirit to enter you, and you shall live;*

⁶ *And I will lay sinews upon you and bring up flesh upon you and cover you with skin, and I will put breath and spirit in you, and you [dry bones] shall live; and you shall know, understand, and realize that I am the Lord [the Sovereign Ruler, Who calls forth loyalty and obedient service].*

MALACHI
Malachi 4:2

² But unto you that fear my name shall the Sun of righteousness arise with healing in his wings; and ye shall go forth, and grow up as calves of the stall.

AMP

² *But unto you who revere and worshipfully fear My name shall the Sun of Righteousness arise with healing in His wings and His beams, and you shall go forth and gambol like calves [released] from the stall and leap for joy.*

Chapter 2

NEW TESTAMENT HEALING SCRIPTURES

MATTHEW
Matthew 8:2-3

2   And, behold, there came a leper and worshipped him, saying, Lord, if thou wilt, thou canst make me clean.

3   And Jesus put forth *his* hand, and touched him, saying, I will; be thou clean. And immediately his leprosy was cleansed.

AMP

2   *And behold, a leper came up to Him and, prostrating himself, worshiped Him, saying, Lord, if You are willing, You are able to cleanse me by curing me.*

3   *And He reached out His hand and touched him, saying, I am willing; be cleansed by being cured. And instantly his leprosy was cured and cleansed.*

Matthew 8:13-15

13   And Jesus said unto the centurion, Go thy way; and as thou hast believed, so be it done unto thee. And his servant was healed in the selfsame hour.

14   And when Jesus was come into Peter's house, he saw his wife's mother laid, and sick of a fever.

15   And he touched her hand, and the fever left her: and she arose, and ministered unto them.

AMP

13   *Then to the centurion Jesus said, Go; it shall be done for you as you have believed. And the servant boy was restored to health at that very moment.*

14   And when Jesus went into Peter's house, He saw his mother-in-law lying ill with a fever.
15   He touched her hand and the fever left her; and she got up and began waiting on Him.

Matthew 8:16-17

16   When the even was come, they brought unto him many that were possessed with devils: and he cast out the spirits with *his* word, and healed all that were sick:

17   That it might be fulfilled which was spoken by Esaias the prophet, saying, Himself took our infirmities, and bare *our* sicknesses.

AMP

16   When evening came, they brought to Him many who were under the power of demons, and He drove out the spirits with a word and restored to health all who were sick.

17   And thus He fulfilled what was spoken by the prophet Isaiah, He Himself took [in order to carry away] our weaknesses and infirmities and bore away our diseases.

Matthew 9:20-21

20   And, behold, a woman, which was diseased with an issue of blood twelve years, came behind *him*, and touched the hem of his garment:

21   For she said within herself, If I may but touch his garment, I shall be whole.

20 *And behold, a woman who had suffered from a flow of blood for twelve years came up behind Him and touched the fringe of His garment;*

21 *For she kept saying to herself, If I only touch His garment, I shall be restored to health.*

Matthew 9: 23-25

23 And when Jesus came into the ruler's house, and saw the minstrels and the people making a noise,

24 He said unto them, Give place: for the maid is not dead, but sleepeth. And they laughed him to scorn.

25 But when the people were put forth, he went in, and took her by the hand, and the maid arose.

AMP

23 *And when Jesus came to the ruler's house and saw the flute players and the crowd making an uproar and din,*

24 *He said, Go away; for the girl is not dead but sleeping. And they laughed and jeered at Him.*

25 *But when the crowd had been ordered to go outside, He went in and took her by the hand, and the girl arose.*

Matthew 9: 27-30

27 And when Jesus departed thence, two blind men followed him, crying, and saying, Thou son of David, have mercy on us.

²⁸ And when he was come into the house, the blind men came to him: and Jesus saith unto them, Believe ye that I am able to do this? They said unto him, Yea, Lord.

²⁹ Then touched he their eyes, saying, According to your faith be it unto you.

³⁰ And their eyes were opened; and Jesus straitly charged them, saying, See that no man know it.

AMP

²⁷ *As Jesus passed on from there, two blind men followed Him, shouting loudly, Have pity and mercy on us, Son of David!*

²⁸ *When He reached the house and went in, the blind men came to Him, and Jesus said to them, Do you believe that I am able to do this? They said to Him, Yes, Lord.*

²⁹ *Then He touched their eyes, saying, According to your faith and trust and reliance [on the power invested in Me] be it done to you;*

³⁰ *And their eyes were opened. And Jesus earnestly and sternly charged them, See that you let no one know about this.*

Matthew 11: 4-6

⁴ Jesus answered and said unto them, Go and shew John again those things which ye do hear and see:

⁵ The blind receive their sight, and the lame walk, the lepers are cleansed, and the deaf hear, the dead are raised up, and the poor have the gospel preached to them.

⁶ And blessed is he, whosoever shall not be offended in me.

⁴   *And Jesus replied to them, Go and report to John what you hear and see:*

⁵   *The blind receive their sight and the lame walk, lepers are cleansed (by healing) and the deaf hear, the dead are raised up and the poor have good news (the Gospel) preached to them.*

⁶   *And blessed (happy, fortunate, and to be envied) is he who takes no offense at Me and finds no cause for stumbling in or through Me and is not hindered from seeing the Truth.*

Matthew 12: 10-13

¹⁰   And, behold there was a man which had *his* hand withered. And they asked him, saying, Is it lawful to heal on the Sabbath days? that they might accuse him.

¹¹   And he said unto them, What man shall there be among you, that shall have one sheep, and if it fall into a pit on the Sabbath day, will he not lay hold on it, and lift it out?

¹²   How much then is a man better than a sheep? Wherefore it is lawful to do well on the Sabbath days.

¹³   Then saith he to the man, Stretch forth thine hand. And he stretched it forth; and it was restored whole, like as the other.

AMP

¹⁰   *And behold, a man was there with one withered hand. And they said to Him, Is it lawful or allowable to cure people on the Sabbath days? -that they might accuse Him.*

¹¹   *But He said to them, What man is there among you, if he has only one sheep and it falls into a pit or ditch on the Sabbath, will not take hold of it and lift it out?*

12   How much better and of more value is a man than a sheep! So it is lawful and allowable to do good on the Sabbath days.

13   Then He said to the man, Reach out your hand. And the man reached it out and it was restored, as sound as the other one.

Matthew 13: 57-58

57   And they were offended in him. But Jesus said unto them, A prophet is not without honour, save in his own country, and in his own house.

58   And he did not many mighty works there because of their unbelief.

AMP

57   And they took offense at Him [they were repelled and hindered from acknowledging His authority, and caused to stumble]. But Jesus said to them, A prophet is not without honor except in his own country and in his own house.

58   And He did not do many works of power there, because of their unbelief (their lack of faith in the divine mission of Jesus).

Matthew 15: 22, 25, 28

22   And, behold, a woman of Canaan came out of the same coasts, and cried unto him, saying, Have mercy on me, O Lord, thou son of David; my daughter is grievously vexed with a devil.

25   Then came she and worshipped him, saying, Lord, help me.

28 Then Jesus answered and said unto her, O woman, great is thy faith: be it unto thee even as thou wilt. And her daughter was made whole from that very hour.

AMP

22 And behold, a woman who was a Canaanite from that district came out and, with a [loud, troublesomely urgent] cry, begged, Have mercy on me, O Lord, Son of David! My daughter is miserably and distressingly and cruelly possessed by a demon!

25 But she came and, kneeling, worshiped Him and kept praying, Lord, help me!

28 Then Jesus answered her, O woman, great is your faith! Be it done for you as you wish. And her daughter was cured from that moment.

Matthew 16:19

19 And I will give unto thee the keys of the kingdom of heaven: and whatsoever thou shalt bind on earth shall be bound in heaven: and whatsoever thou shalt loose on earth shall be loosed in heaven.

AMP

19 I will give you the keys of the kingdom of heaven; and whatever you bind (declare to be improper and unlawful) on earth must be what is already bound in heaven; and whatever you loose (declare lawful) on earth must be what is already loosed in heaven.

Matthew 17: 18, 20-21

[18] And Jesus rebuked the devil; and he departed out of him: and the child was cured from that very hour.

[20] And Jesus said unto them, Because of your unbelief: for verily I say unto you, If ye have faith as a grain of mustard seed, ye shall say unto this mountain, Remove hence to yonder place; and it shall remove; and nothing shall be impossible unto you.

[21] Howbeit this kind goeth not out but by prayer and fasting.

AMP

[18] *And Jesus rebuked the demon, and it came out of him, and the boy was cured instantly.*

[20] *He said to them, Because of the littleness of your faith [that is, your lack of firmly relying trust]. For truly I say to you, if you have faith [that is living] like a grain of mustard seed, you can say to this mountain, Move from here to yonder place, and it will move; and nothing will be impossible to you.*

[21] *But this kind does not go out except by prayer and fasting.*

Matthew 18: 18-20

[18] Verily I say unto you, Whatsoever ye shall bind on earth shall be bound in heaven: and whatsoever ye shall loose on earth shall be loosed in heaven.

[19] Again I say unto you, That if two of you shall agree on earth as touching any thing that they shall ask, it shall be done for them of my Father which is in heaven.

20   For where two or three are gathered together in my name, there am I in the midst of them.

AMP

18   Truly I tell you, whatever you forbid and declare to be improper and unlawful on earth must be what is already forbidden in heaven, and whatever you permit and declare proper and lawful on earth must be what is already permitted in heaven.

19   Again I tell you, if two of you on earth agree (harmonize together, make a symphony together) about whatever [anything and everything] they may ask, it will come to pass and be done for them by My Father in heaven.

20   For wherever two or three are gathered (drawn together as My followers) in (into) My name, there I AM in the midst of them.

Matthew 20: 30-34

30   And, behold, two blind men sitting by the way side, when they heard that Jesus passed by, cried out, saying, Have mercy on us, O Lord, thou son of David.

31   And the multitude rebuked them, because they should hold their peace: but they cried the more, saying, Have mercy on us, O Lord, thou son of David.

32   And Jesus stood still, and called them, and said, What will ye that I shall do unto you?

33   They say unto him, Lord, that our eyes may be opened.

34   So Jesus had compassion on them, and touched their eyes: and immediately their eyes received sight, and they followed him.

30 *And behold, two blind men were sitting by the roadside, and when they heard that Jesus was passing by, they cried out, Lord, have pity and mercy on us, [You] Son of David!*

31 *The crowds reproved them and told them to keep still; but they cried out all the more, Lord, have pity and mercy on us, [You] Son of David!*

32 *And Jesus stopped and called them, and asked, What do you want Me to do for you?*

33 *They answered Him, Lord, we want our eyes to be opened!*

34 *And Jesus, in pity, touched their eyes; and instantly they received their sight and followed Him.*

MARK
Mark 1: 32-34

32 And at even, when the sun did set, they brought unto him all that were diseased, and them that were possessed with devils.

33 And all the city was gathered together at the door.

34 And he healed many that were sick of divers diseases, and cast out many devils; and suffered not the devils to speak, because they knew him.

AMP

32 *Now when it was evening, after the sun had set, they brought to Him all who were sick and those under the power of demons,*

33 *Until the whole town was gathered together about the door.*

³⁴ *And He cured many who were afflicted with various diseases; and He drove out many demons, but would not allow the demons to talk because they knew Him intuitively].*

Mark 7: 31-35

³¹   And again, departing from the coasts of Tyre and Sidon, he came unto the Sea of Galilee, through the midst of the coasts of Decapolis.

³²   And they bring unto him one that was deaf, and had an impediment in his speech; and they beseech him to put his hand upon him.

³³   And he took him aside from the multitude, and put his fingers into his ears, and he spit, and touched his tongue;

³⁴   And looking up to heaven, he sighed, and saith unto him, Ephphatha, that is, Be opened.

³⁵   And straightway his ears were opened, and the string of his tongue was loosed, and he spake plain.

AMP

³¹   *Soon after this, Jesus, coming back from the region of Tyre, passed through Sidon on to the Sea of Galilee, through the region of Decapolis [the ten cities].*

³²   *And they brought to Him a man who was deaf and had difficulty in speaking, and they begged Jesus to place His hand upon him.*

³³   *And taking him aside from the crowd [privately], He thrust His fingers into the man's ears and spat and touched his tongue;*

³⁴   *And looking up to heaven, He sighed as He said, Ephphatha, which means, Be opened!*

³⁵   *And his ears were opened, his tongue was loosed, and he began to speak distinctly and as he should.*

Mark 8: 22-25

22 And he cometh to Bethsaida; and they bring a blind man unto him, and besought him to touch him.

23 And he took the blind man by the hand, and led him out of the town; and when he had spit on his eyes, and put his hands upon him, he asked him if he saw ought.

24 And he looked up, and said, I see men as trees, walking.

25 After that he put his hands again upon his eyes, and made him look up: and he was restored, and saw every man clearly.

AMP

22 *And they came to Bethsaida. And [people] brought to Him a blind man and begged Him to touch him.*

23 *And He caught the blind man by the hand and led him out of the village; and when He had spit on his eyes and put His hands upon him, He asked him, Do you possibly] see anything?*

24 *And he looked up and said, I see people, but [they look] like trees, walking.*

25 *Then He put His hands on his eyes again; and the man looked intently [that is, fixed his eyes on definite objects], and he was restored and saw everything distinctly [even what was at a distance].*

Mark 16: 17-18

17 And these signs shall follow them that believe; In my name shall they cast out devils; they shall speak with new tongues;

¹⁸ They shall take up serpents; and if they drink any deadly thing, it shall not hurt them; they shall lay hands on the sick, and they shall recover.

AMP

¹⁷ *And these attesting signs will accompany those who believe: in My name they will drive out demons; they will speak in new languages;*

¹⁸ *They will pick up serpents; and [even] if they drink anything deadly, it will not hurt them; they will lay their hands on the sick, and they will get well.*

LUKE
Luke 4: 18-19

¹⁸ The Spirit of the Lord is upon me, because he hath anointed me to preach the gospel to the poor; he hath sent me to heal the brokenhearted, to preach deliverance to the captives, and recovering of sight to the blind, to set at liberty them that are bruised,

¹⁹ To preach the acceptable year of the Lord.

AMP

¹⁸ *The Spirit of the Lord [is] upon Me, because He has anointed Me [the Anointed One, the Messiah] to preach the good news (the Gospel) to the poor; He has sent Me to announce release to the captives and recovery of sight to the blind, to send forth as delivered those who are oppressed [who are downtrodden, bruised, crushed, and broken down by calamity],*

¹⁹ *To proclaim the accepted and acceptable year of the Lord [the day when salvation and the free favors of God profusely abound].*

Luke 5: 15-17

15   But so much the more went there a fame abroad of him: and great multitudes came together to hear, and to be healed by him of their infirmities.

16   And he withdrew himself into the wilderness, and prayed.

17   And it came to pass on a certain day, as he was teaching, that there were Pharisees and doctors of the law sitting by, which were come out of every town of Galilee, and Judaea, and Jerusalem: and the power of the Lord was present to heal them.

AMP

15   *But so much the more the news spread abroad concerning Him, and great crowds kept coming together to hear [Him] and to be healed by Him of their infirmities.*

16   *But He Himself withdrew [in retirement] to the wilderness (desert) and prayed.*

17   *One of those days, as He was teaching, there were Pharisees and teachers of the Law sitting by, who had come from every village and town of Galilee and Judea and from Jerusalem. And the power of the Lord was [present] with Him to heal them.*

Luke 5: 18-25

18   And, behold, men brought in a bed a man which was taken with a palsy: and they sought means to bring him in, and to lay him before him.

19   And when they could not find by what way they might bring him in because of the multitude, they went upon the housetop, and let him down through the tiling with his couch into the midst before Jesus.

20   And when he saw their faith, he said unto him, Man, thy sins are forgiven thee.

21   And the scribes and the Pharisees began to reason, saying, Who is this which speaketh blasphemies? Who can forgive sins, but God alone?

22   But when Jesus perceived their thoughts, he answering said unto them, What reason ye in your hearts?

23   Whether is easier, to say, Thy sins be forgiven thee; or to say, Rise up and walk?

24   But that ye may know that the Son of man hath power upon earth to forgive sins, (he said unto the sick of the palsy,) I say unto thee, Arise, and take up thy couch, and go into thine house.

25   And immediately he rose up before them, and took up that whereon he lay, and departed to his own house, glorifying God.

AMP

18   *And behold, some men were bringing on a stretcher a man who was paralyzed, and they tried to carry him in and lay him before [Jesus].*

19   *But finding no way to bring him in because of the crowd, they went up on the roof and lowered him with his stretcher through the tiles into the midst, in front of Jesus.*

20   *And when He saw [their confidence in Him, springing from] their faith, He said, Man, your sins are forgiven you!*

21   *And the scribes and the Pharisees began to reason and question and argue, saying, Who is this [Man] Who speaks blasphemies? Who can forgive sins but God alone?*

22   *But Jesus, knowing their thoughts and questionings, answered them, Why do you question in your hearts?*

23   *Which is easier: to say, Your sins are forgiven you, or to say, Arise and walk [about]?*

24   *But that you may know that the Son of Man has the [power of] authority and right on earth to forgive sins, He said to the paralyzed man, I say to you, arise, pick up your litter (stretcher), and go to your own house!*

25   *And instantly [the man] stood up before them and picked up what he had been lying on and went away to his house, recognizing and praising and thanking God.*

Luke 7: 6-7

6   Then Jesus went with them. And when he was now not far from the house, the centurion sent friends to him, saying unto him, Lord, trouble not thyself: for I am not worthy that thou shouldest enter under my roof:

7   Wherefore neither thought I myself worthy to come unto thee: but say in a word, and my servant shall be healed.

AMP

6   *And Jesus went with them. But when He was not far from the house, the centurion sent [some] friends to Him, saying, Lord, do not trouble [Yourself], for I am not sufficiently worthy to have You come under my roof;*

7   *Neither did I consider myself worthy to come to You. But [just] speak a word, and my servant boy will be healed.*

Luke 7: 11-15

11   And it came to pass the day after, that he went into a city called Nain; and many of his disciples went with him, and much people.

12   Now when he came nigh to the gate of the city, behold, there was a dead man carried out, the only son of his mother, and she was a widow: and much people of the city was with her.

13   And when the Lord saw her, he had compassion on her, and said unto her, Weep not.

14   And he came and touched the bier: and they that bare him stood still. And he said, Young man, I say unto thee, Arise.

15   And he that was dead sat up, and began to speak. And he delivered him to his mother.

AMP

11   *Soon afterward, Jesus went to a town called Nain, and His disciples and a great throng accompanied Him.*

12   *[Just] as He drew near the gate of the town, behold, a man who had died was being carried out—the only son of his mother, and she was a widow; and a large gathering from the town was accompanying her.*

13   *And when the Lord saw her, He had compassion on her and said to her, Do not weep.*

14   *And He went forward and touched the funeral bier, and the pallbearers stood still. And He said, Young man, I say to you, arise [from death]!*

15   *And the man [who was] dead sat up and began to speak. And [Jesus] gave him [back] to his mother.*

Luke 8: 41-42, 49-51, 54-55

41   And, behold, there came a man named Jairus, and he was a ruler of the synagogue: and he fell down at Jesus' feet, and besought him that he would come into his house:

42   For he had one only daughter, about twelve years of age, and she lay a dying. But as he went the people thronged him.

49   While he yet spake, there cometh one from the ruler of the synagogue's house, saying to him, Thy daughter is dead; trouble not the Master.

50   But when Jesus heard it, he answered him, saying, Fear not: believe only, and she shall be made whole.

51   And when he came into the house, he suffered no man to go in, save Peter, and James, and John, and the father and the mother of the maiden.

54   And he put them all out, and took her by the hand, and called, saying, Maid, arise.

55   And her spirit came again, and she arose straightway: and he commanded to give her meat.

AMP

41   *And there came a man named Jairus, who had [for a long time] been a director of the synagogue; and falling at the feet of Jesus, he begged Him to come to his house,*

⁴² *For he had an only daughter, about twelve years of age, and she was dying. As [Jesus] went, the people pressed together around Him [almost suffocating Him].*

⁴⁹ *While He was still speaking, a man from the house of the director of the synagogue came and said [to Jairus], Your daughter is dead; do not weary and trouble the Teacher any further.*

⁵⁰ *But Jesus, on hearing this, answered him, Do not be seized with alarm or struck with fear; simply believe [in Me as able to do this], and she shall be made well.*

⁵¹ *And when He came to the house, He permitted no one to enter with Him except Peter and John and James, and the girl's father and mother.*

⁵⁴ *And grasping her hand, He called, saying, Child, arise [from the sleep of death]!*

⁵⁵ *And her spirit returned [from death], and she arose immediately; and He directed that she should be given something to eat.*

Luke 7: 43-48

⁴³ And a woman having an issue of blood twelve years, which had spent all her living upon physicians, neither could be healed of any,

⁴⁴ Came behind him, and touched the border of his garment: and immediately her issue of blood stanched.

⁴⁵ And Jesus said, Who touched me? When all denied, Peter and they that were with him said, Master, the multitude throng thee and press thee, and sayest thou, Who touched me?

⁴⁶ And Jesus said, Somebody hath touched me: for I perceive that virtue is gone out of me.

47   And when the woman saw that she was not hid, she came trembling, and falling down before him, she declared unto him before all the people for what cause she had touched him, and how she was healed immediately.

48   And he said unto her, Daughter, be of good comfort: thy faith hath made thee whole; go in peace.

AMP

43   *And a woman who had suffered from a flow of blood for twelve years and had spent all her living upon physicians, and could not be healed by anyone,*

44   *Came up behind Him and touched the fringe of His garment, and immediately her flow of blood ceased.*

45   *And Jesus said, Who is it who touched Me? When all were denying it, Peter and those who were with him said, Master, the multitudes surround You and press You on every side!*

46   *But Jesus said, Someone did touch Me; for I perceived that [healing] power has gone forth from Me.*

47   *And when the woman saw that she had not escaped notice, she came up trembling, and, falling down before Him, she declared in the presence of all the people for what reason she had touched Him and how she had been instantly cured.*

48   *And He said to her, Daughter, your faith (your confidence and trust in Me) has made you well! Go (enter) into peace (untroubled, undisturbed well-being).*

Luke 13: 10-13

10 And he was teaching in one of the synagogues on the Sabbath.

11 And, behold, there was a woman which had a spirit of infirmity eighteen years, and was bowed together, and could in no wise lift up herself.

12 And when Jesus saw her, he called her to him, and said unto her, Woman, thou art loosed from thine infirmity.

13 And he laid his hands on her: and immediately she was made straight, and glorified God.

AMP

10 *Now Jesus was teaching in one of the synagogues on the Sabbath.*

11 *And there was a woman there who for eighteen years had had an infirmity caused by a spirit (a demon of sickness). She was bent completely forward and utterly unable to straighten herself up or to look upward.*

12 *And when Jesus saw her, He called [her to Him] and said to her, Woman, you are released from your infirmity!*

13 *Then He laid [His] hands on her, and instantly she was made straight, and she recognized and thanked and praised God.*

Luke 14: 1-4

1 And it came to pass, as he went into the house of one of the chief Pharisees to eat bread on the Sabbath day, that they watched him.

2   And, behold, there was a certain man before him which had the dropsy.

3   And Jesus answering spake unto the lawyers and Pharisees, saying, Is it lawful to heal on the Sabbath day?

4   And they held their peace. And he took him, and healed him, and let him go;

AMP

1   It occurred one Sabbath, when [Jesus] went for a meal at the house of one of the ruling Pharisees, that they were [engaged in] watching Him [closely].

2   And behold, [just] in front of Him there was a man who had dropsy.

3   And Jesus asked the lawyers and the Pharisees, Is it lawful and right to cure on the Sabbath or not?

4   But they kept silent. Then He took hold [of the man] and cured him and sent him away.

Luke 17: 12-19

12   And as he entered into a certain village, there met him ten men that were lepers, which stood
afar off:

13   And they lifted up their voices, and said, Jesus, Master, have mercy on us.

14   And when he saw them, he said unto them, Go shew yourselves unto the priests. And it came to pass, that, as they went, they were cleansed.

15   And one of them, when he saw that he was healed, turned back, and with a loud voice glorified God,

¹⁶ And fell down on his face at his feet, giving him thanks: and he was a Samaritan.

¹⁷ And Jesus answering said, Were there not ten cleansed? but where are the nine?

¹⁸ There are not found that returned to give glory to God, save this stranger.

¹⁹ And he said unto him, Arise, go thy way: thy faith hath made thee whole.

AMP

¹² *And as He was going into one village, He was met by ten lepers, who stood at a distance.*

¹³ *And they raised up their voices and called, Jesus, Master, take pity and have mercy on us!*

¹⁴ *And when He saw them, He said to them, Go [at once] and show yourselves to the priests. And as they went, they were cured and made clean.*

¹⁵ *Then one of them, upon seeing that he was cured, turned back, recognizing and thanking and praising God with a loud voice;*

¹⁶ *And he fell prostrate at Jesus' feet, thanking Him [over and over]. And he was a Samaritan.*

¹⁷ *Then Jesus asked, Were not [all] ten cleansed? Where are the nine?*

¹⁸ *Was there no one found to return and to recognize and give thanks and praise to God except this alien?*

¹⁹ *And He said to him, Get up and go on your way. Your faith (your trust and confidence that spring from your belief in God) has restored you to health.*

Luke 22: 49-51

⁴⁹ When they which were about him saw what would follow, they said unto him, Lord, shall we smite with the sword?

⁵⁰ And one of them smote the servant of the high priest, and cut off his right ear.

⁵¹ And Jesus answered and said, Suffer ye thus far. And he touched his ear, and healed him.

AMP

⁴⁹ *And when those who were around Him saw what was about to happen, they said, Lord, shall we strike with the sword?*

⁵⁰ *And one of them struck the bond servant of the high priest and cut off his ear, the right one.*

⁵¹ *But Jesus said, Permit them to go so far [as to seize Me]. And He touched the little (insignificant) ear and healed him.*

JOHN
John 3: 14-15

¹⁴ And as Moses lifted up the serpent in the wilderness, even so must the Son of man be lifted up:

¹⁵ That whosoever believeth in him should not perish, but have eternal life.

AMP

¹⁴ *And just as Moses lifted up the serpent in the desert [on a pole], so must [so it is necessary that] the Son of Man be lifted up [on the cross],*

¹⁵ *In order that everyone who believes in Him [who cleaves to Him, trusts Him, and relies on Him] may not perish, but have eternal life and [actually] live forever!*

John 4: 13-14

[13] Jesus answered and said unto her, Whosoever drinketh of this water shall thirst again:

[14] But whosoever drinketh of the water that I shall give him shall never thirst; but the water that I shall give him shall be in him a well of water springing up into everlasting life.

AMP

[13] *Jesus answered her, All who drink of this water will be thirsty again.*

[14] *But whoever takes a drink of the water that I will give him shall never, no never, be thirsty any more. But the water that I will give him shall become a spring of water welling up (flowing, bubbling) [continually] within him unto (into, for) eternal life.*

John 4: 46-53

[46] So Jesus came again into Cana of Galilee, where he made the water wine. And there was a certain nobleman, whose son was sick at Capernaum.

[47] When he heard that Jesus was come out of Judaea into Galilee, he went unto him, and besought him that he would come down, and heal his son: for he was at the point of death.

[48] Then said Jesus unto him, Except ye see signs and wonders, ye will not believe.

[49] The nobleman saith unto him, Sir, come down ere my child die.

[50] Jesus saith unto him, Go thy way; thy son liveth. And the man believed the word that Jesus had spoken unto him, and he went his way.

51 And as he was now going down, his servants met him, and told him, saying, Thy son liveth.

52 Then enquired he of them the hour when he began to amend. And they said unto him, Yesterday at the seventh hour the fever left him.

53 So the father knew that it was at the same hour, in the which Jesus said unto him, Thy son liveth: and himself believed, and his whole house.

AMP

46 *So Jesus came again to Cana of Galilee, where He had turned the water into wine. And there was a certain royal official whose son was lying ill in Capernaum.*

47 *Having heard that Jesus had come back from Judea into Galilee, he went away to meet Him and began to beg Him to come down and cure his son, for he was lying at the point of death.*

48 *Then Jesus said to him, Unless you see signs and miracles happen, you [people] never will believe (trust, have faith) at all.*

49 *The king's officer pleaded with Him, Sir, do come down at once before my little child is dead!*

50 *Jesus answered him, Go in peace; your son will live! And the man put his trust in what Jesus said and started home.*

51 *But even as he was on the road going down, his servants met him and reported, saying, Your son lives!*

52 *So he asked them at what time he had begun to get better. They said, Yesterday during the seventh hour (about one o'clock in the afternoon) the fever left him.*

53 *Then the father knew that it was at that very hour when Jesus had said to him, Your son will live. And he and his entire household believed (adhered to, trusted in, and relied on Jesus).*

John 5: 2-9

2 Now there is at Jerusalem by the sheep market a pool, which is called in the Hebrew tongue Bethesda, having five porches.

3 In these lay a great multitude of impotent folk, of blind, halt, withered, waiting for the moving of the water.

4 For an angel went down at a certain season into the pool, and troubled the water: whosoever then first after the troubling of the water stepped in was made whole of whatsoever disease he had.

5 And a certain man was there, which had an infirmity thirty and eight years.

6 When Jesus saw him lie, and knew that he had been now a long time in that case, he saith unto him, Wilt thou be made whole?

7 The impotent man answered him, Sir, I have no man, when the water is troubled, to put me into the pool: but while I am coming, another steppeth down before me.

8 Jesus saith unto him, Rise, take up thy bed, and walk.

9 And immediately the man was made whole, and took up his bed, and walked: and on the same day was the Sabbath.

2   Now there is in Jerusalem a pool near the Sheep Gate. This pool in the Hebrew is called Bethesda, having five porches (alcoves, colonnades, doorways).

3   In these lay a great number of sick folk—some blind, some crippled, and some paralyzed (shriveled up) - waiting for the bubbling up of the water.

4   For an angel of the Lord went down at appointed seasons into the pool and moved and stirred up the water; whoever then first, after the stirring up of the water, stepped in was cured of whatever disease with which he was afflicted.

5   There was a certain man there who had suffered with a deep-seated and lingering disorder for thirty-eight years.

6   When Jesus noticed him lying there [helpless], knowing that he had already been a long time in that condition, He said to him, Do you want to become well? [Are you really in earnest about getting well?]

7   The invalid answered, Sir, I have nobody when the water is moving to put me into the pool; but while I am trying to come [into it] myself, somebody else steps down ahead of me.

8   Jesus said to him, Get up! Pick up your bed (sleeping pad) and walk!

9   Instantly the man became well and recovered his strength and picked up his bed and walked. But that happened on the Sabbath.

John 10: 9-10

9   I am the door: by me if any man enter in, he shall be saved, and shall go in and out, and find pasture.

10 The thief cometh not, but for to steal, and to kill, and to destroy: I am come that they might have life, and that they might have it more abundantly.

AMP

9 I am the Door; anyone who enters in through Me will be saved (will live). He will come in and he will go out [freely], and will find pasture.

10 The thief comes only in order to steal and kill and destroy. I came that they may have and enjoy life, and have it in abundance (to the full, till it overflows).

John 11: 25-26

25 Jesus said unto her, I am the resurrection, and the life: he that believeth in me, though he were dead, yet shall he live:

26 And whosoever liveth and believeth in me shall never die. Believest thou this?

AMP

25 Jesus said to her, I am [Myself] the Resurrection and the Life. Whoever believes in (adheres to, trusts in, and relies on) Me, although he may die, yet he shall live;

26 And whoever continues to live and believes in (has faith in, cleaves to, and relies on) Me shall never [actually] die at all. Do you believe this?

John 11: 40-44

40 Jesus saith unto her, Said I not unto thee, that, if thou wouldest believe, thou shouldest see the glory of God?

41 Then they took away the stone from the place where the dead was laid. And Jesus lifted up his eyes, and said, Father, I thank thee that thou hast heard me.

42 And I knew that thou hearest me always: but because of the people which stand by I said it, that they may believe that thou hast sent me.

43 And when he thus had spoken, he cried with a loud voice, Lazarus, come forth.

44 And he that was dead came forth, bound hand and foot with graveclothes: and his face was bound about with a napkin. Jesus saith unto them, Loose him, and let him go.

AMP

40 *Jesus said to her, Did I not tell you and promise you that if you would believe and rely on Me, you would see the glory of God?*

41 *So they took away the stone. And Jesus lifted up His eyes and said, Father, I thank You that You have heard Me.*

42 *Yes, I know You always hear and listen to Me, but I have said this on account of and for the benefit of the people standing around, so that they may believe that You did send Me [that You have made Me Your Messenger].*

43 *When He had said this, He shouted with a loud voice, Lazarus, come out!*

44 *And out walked the man who had been dead, his hands and feet wrapped in burial cloths (linen strips), and with a [burial] napkin bound around his face. Jesus said to them, Free him of the burial wrappings and let him go.*

ACTS
Acts 5: 12-16

¹² And by the hands of the apostles were many signs and wonders wrought among the people; (and they were all with one accord in Solomon's porch.

¹³ And of the rest durst no man join himself to them: but the people magnified them.

¹⁴ And believers were the more added to the Lord, multitudes both of men and women.)

¹⁵ Insomuch that they brought forth the sick into the streets, and laid them on beds and couches, that at the least the shadow of Peter passing by might overshadow some of them.

¹⁶ There came also a multitude out of the cities round about unto Jerusalem, bringing sick folks, and them which were vexed with unclean spirits: and they were healed every one.

AMP

¹² *Now by the hands of the apostles (special messengers) numerous and startling signs and wonders were being performed among the people. And by common consent they all met together [at the temple] in the covered porch (walk) called Solomon's.*

¹³ *And none of those who were not of their number dared to join and associate with them, but the people held them in high regard and praised and made much of them.*

¹⁴ *More and more there were being added to the Lord those who believed [those who acknowledged Jesus as their Savior and devoted themselves to Him joined and gathered with them], crowds both of men and of women,*

15   *So that they [even] kept carrying out the sick into the streets and placing them on couches and sleeping pads, [in the hope] that as Peter passed by, at least his shadow might fall on some of them.*

16   *And the people gathered also from the towns and hamlets around Jerusalem, bringing the sick and those troubled with foul spirits, and they were all cured.*

Acts 8: 5-8

5   Then Philip went down to the city of Samaria, and preached Christ unto them.

6   And the people with one accord gave heed unto those things which Philip spake, hearing and seeing the miracles which he did.

7   For unclean spirits, crying with loud voice, came out of many that were possessed with them: and many taken with palsies, and that were lame, were healed.

8   And there was great joy in that city.

AMP

5   *Philip [the deacon, not the apostle] went down to the city of Samaria and proclaimed the Christ (the Messiah) to them [the people];*

6   *And great crowds of people with one accord listened to and heeded what was said by Philip, as they heard him and watched the miracles and wonders which he kept performing [from time to time].*

7   *For foul spirits came out of many who were possessed by them, screaming and shouting with a loud voice, and many who were suffering from palsy or were crippled were restored to health.*

8   *And there was great rejoicing in that city.*

Acts 19: 11-12

11   And God wrought special miracles by the hands of Paul:

12   So that from his body were brought unto the sick handkerchiefs or aprons, and the diseases departed from them, and the evil spirits went out of them.

AMP

11   *And God did unusual and extraordinary miracles by the hands of Paul,*

12   *So that handkerchiefs or towels or aprons which had touched his skin were carried away and put upon the sick, and their diseases left them and the evil spirits came out of them.*

ROMANS
Romans 5: 12-21

12   Wherefore, as by one man sin entered into the world, and death by sin; and so death passed upon all men, for that all have sinned:

13   (For until the law sin was in the world: but sin is not imputed when there is no law.

14   Nevertheless death reigned from Adam to Moses, even over them that had not sinned after the similitude of Adam's transgression, who is the figure of him that was to come.

15   But not as the offence, so also is the free gift. For if through the offence of one many be dead, much more the grace of God, and the gift by grace, which is by one man, Jesus Christ, hath abounded unto many.

16   And not as it was by one that sinned, so is the gift: for the judgment was by one to condemnation, but the free gift is of many offences unto justification.

17 For if by one man's offence death reigned by one; much more they which receive abundance of grace and of the gift of righteousness shall reign in life by one, Jesus Christ.)

18 Therefore as by the offence of one judgment came upon all men to condemnation; even so by the righteousness of one the free gift came upon all men unto justification of life.

19 For as by one man's disobedience many were made sinners, so by the obedience of one shall many be made righteous.

20 Moreover the law entered, that the offence might abound. But where sin abounded, grace did much more abound:

21 That as sin hath reigned unto death, even so might grace reign through righteousness unto eternal life by Jesus Christ our Lord.

AMP

12 Therefore, as sin came into the world through one man, and death as the result of sin, so death spread to all men [no one being able to stop it or to escape its power] because all men sinned.

13 [To be sure] sin was in the world before ever the Law was given, but sin is not charged to men's account where there is no law [to transgress].

14 Yet death held sway from Adam to Moses [the Lawgiver], even over those who did not themselves transgress [a positive command] as Adam did. Adam was a type (prefigure) of the One Who was to come [in reverse, the former destructive, the Latter saving].

15   But God's free gift is not at all to be compared to the trespass [His grace is out of all proportion to the fall of man]. For if many died through one man's falling away (his lapse, his offense), much more profusely did God's grace and the free gift [that comes] through the undeserved favor of the one Man Jesus Christ abound and overflow to and for [the benefit of] many.

16   Nor is the free gift at all to be compared to the effect of that one [man's] sin. For the sentence [following the trespass] of one [man] brought condemnation, whereas the free gift [following] many transgressions brings justification (an act of righteousness).

17   For if because of one man's trespass (lapse, offense) death reigned through that one, much more surely will those who receive [God's] overflowing grace (unmerited favor) and the free gift of righteousness [putting them into right standing with Himself] reign as kings in life through the one Man Jesus Christ (the Messiah, the Anointed One).

18   Well then, as one man's trespass [one man's false step and falling away led] to condemnation for all men, so one Man's act of righteousness [leads] to acquittal and right standing with God and life for all men.

19   For just as by one man's disobedience (failing to hear, heedlessness, and carelessness) the many were constituted sinners, so by one Man's obedience the many will be constituted righteous (made acceptable to God, brought into right standing with Him).

20   But then Law came in, [only] to expand and increase the trespass [making it more apparent

and exciting opposition]. *But where sin increased and abounded, grace (God's unmerited favor) has surpassed it and increased the more and superabounded,*

21 *So that, [just] as sin has reigned in death, [so] grace (His unearned and undeserved favor) might reign also through righteousness (right standing with God) which issues in eternal life through Jesus Christ (the Messiah, the Anointed One) our Lord.*

Romans 8: 8-16

8 So then they that are in the flesh cannot please God.

9 But ye are not in the flesh, but in the Spirit, if so be that the Spirit of God dwell in you. Now if any man have not the Spirit of Christ, he is none of his.

10 And if Christ be in you, the body is dead because of sin; but the Spirit is life because of righteousness.

11 But if the Spirit of him that raised up Jesus from the dead dwell in you, he that raised up Christ from the dead shall also quicken your mortal bodies by his Spirit that dwelleth in you.

12 Therefore, brethren, we are debtors, not to the flesh, to live after the flesh.

13 For if ye live after the flesh, ye shall die: but if ye through the Spirit do mortify the deeds of the body, ye shall live.

14 For as many as are led by the Spirit of God, they are the sons of God.

15 For ye have not received the spirit of bondage again to fear; but ye have received the Spirit of adoption, whereby we cry, Abba, Father.

¹⁶ The Spirit itself beareth witness with our spirit, that we are the children of God:

AMP

⁸ *So then those who are living the life of the flesh [catering to the appetites and impulses of their carnal nature] cannot please or satisfy God, or be acceptable to Him.*

⁹ *But you are not living the life of the flesh, you are living the life of the Spirit, if the [Holy] Spirit of God [really] dwells within you [directs and controls you]. But if anyone does not possess the [Holy] Spirit of Christ, he is none of His [he does not belong to Christ, is not truly a child of God].*

¹⁰ *But if Christ lives in you, [then although] your [natural] body is dead by reason of sin and guilt, the spirit is alive because of [the] righteousness [that He imputes to you].*

¹¹ *And if the Spirit of Him Who raised up Jesus from the dead dwells in you, [then] He Who raised up Christ Jesus from the dead will also restore to life your mortal (short-lived, perishable) bodies through His Spirit Who dwells in you.*

¹² *So then, brethren, we are debtors, but not to the flesh [we are not obligated to our carnal nature], to live [a life ruled by the standards set up by the dictates] of the flesh.*

¹³ *For if you live according to [the dictates of] the flesh, you will surely die. But if through the power of the [Holy] Spirit you are [habitually] putting to death (making extinct, deadening) the [evil] deeds prompted by the body, you shall [really and genuinely] live forever.*

¹⁴ *For all who are led by the Spirit of God are sons of God.*

15   For [the Spirit which] you have now received [is] not a spirit of slavery to put you once more in bondage to fear, but you have received the Spirit of adoption [the Spirit producing sonship] in [the bliss of] which we cry, Abba (Father)! Father!

16   The Spirit Himself [thus] testifies together with our own spirit, [assuring us] that we are children of God.

Romans 10: 8-17

8   But what saith it? The word is nigh thee, even in thy mouth, and in thy heart: that is, the word of faith, which we preach;

9   That if thou shalt confess with thy mouth the Lord Jesus, and shalt believe in thine heart that God hath raised him from the dead, thou shalt be saved.

10   For with the heart man believeth unto righteousness; and with the mouth confession is made unto salvation.

11   For the scripture saith, Whosoever believeth on him shall not be ashamed.

12   For there is no difference between the Jew and the Greek: for the same Lord over all is rich unto all that call upon him.

13   For whosoever shall call upon the name of the Lord shall be saved.

14   How then shall they call on him in whom they have not believed? and how shall they believe in him of whom they have not heard? and how shall they hear without a preacher?

¹⁵   And how shall they preach, except they be sent? as it is written, How beautiful are the feet of them that preach the gospel of peace, and bring glad   tidings of good things!

¹⁶   But they have not all obeyed the gospel. For Esaias saith, Lord, who hath believed our report?

¹⁷   So then faith cometh by hearing, and hearing by the word of God.

AMP

⁸   *But what does it say? The Word (God's message in Christ) is near you, on your lips and in your heart; that is, the Word (the message, the basis and object) of faith which we preach,*

⁹   *Because if you acknowledge and confess with your lips that Jesus is Lord and in your heart believe (adhere to, trust in, and rely on the truth) that God raised Him from the dead, you will be saved.*

¹⁰   *For with the heart a person believes (adheres to, trusts in, and relies on Christ) and so is justified (declared righteous, acceptable to God), and with the mouth he confesses (declares openly and speaks out freely his faith) and confirms [his] salvation.*

¹¹   *The Scripture says, No man who believes in Him [who adheres to, relies on, and trusts in Him] will [ever] be put to shame or be disappointed.*

¹²   *[No one] for there is no distinction between Jew and Greek. The same Lord is Lord over all [of us] and He generously bestows His riches upon all who call upon Him [in faith].*

¹³   *For everyone who calls upon the name of the Lord [invoking Him as Lord] will be saved.*

14   But how are people to call upon Him Whom they have not believed [in Whom they have no faith, on Whom they have no reliance]? And how are they to believe in Him [adhere to, trust in, and rely   upon Him] of Whom they have never heard? And how are they to hear without a preacher?

15   And how can men [be expected to] preach unless they are sent? As it is written, How beautiful are the feet of those who bring glad tidings! [How welcome is the coming of those who preach the good news of His good things!]

16   But they have not all heeded the Gospel; for Isaiah says, Lord, who has believed (had faith in) what he has heard from us?

17   So faith comes by hearing [what is told], and what is heard comes by the preaching [of the message that came from the lips] of Christ (the Messiah Himself).

1 CORINTHIANS
1 Corinthians 15:20-22

20   But now is Christ risen from the dead, and become the firstfruits of them that slept.

21   For since by man came death, by man came also the resurrection of the dead.

22   For as in Adam all die, even so in Christ shall all be made alive.

AMP

20   But the fact is that Christ (the Messiah) has been raised from the dead, and He became the firstfruits of those who have fallen asleep [in death].

21   For since [it was] through a man that death [came into the world, it is] also through a Man that the resurrection of the dead [has come].

²² *For just as [because of their union of nature] in Adam all people die, so also [by virtue of their union of nature] shall all in Christ be made alive.*

<u>EPHESIANS</u>
Ephesians 1:20-23

²⁰ Which he wrought in Christ, when he raised him from the dead, and set him at his own right hand in the heavenly places,

²¹ Far above all principality, and power, and might, and dominion, and every name that is named, not only in this world, but also in that which is to come:

²² And hath put all things under his feet, and gave him to be the head over all things to the church,

²³ Which is his body, the fulness of him that filleth all in all.

AMP

²⁰ *Which He exerted in Christ when He raised Him from the dead and seated Him at His [own] right hand in the heavenly [places],*

²¹ *Far above all rule and authority and power and dominion and every name that is named [above every title that can be conferred], not only in this age and in this world, but also in the age and the world which are to come.*

²² *And He has put all things under His feet and has appointed Him the universal and supreme Head of the church [a headship exercised throughout the church],*

23 *Which is His body, the fullness of Him Who fills all in all [for in that body lives the full measure of Him Who makes everything complete, and Who fills everything everywhere with Himself].*

HEBREWS
Hebrews 4:16
16 Let us therefore come boldly unto the throne of grace, that we may obtain mercy, and find grace to help in time of need.
AMP
16 *Let us then fearlessly and confidently and boldly draw near to the throne of grace (the throne of God's unmerited favor to us sinners), that we may receive mercy [for our failures] and find grace to help in good time for every need [appropriate help and well-timed help, coming just when we need it].*

JAMES
James 5:13-16
13 Is any among you afflicted? let him pray. Is any merry? let him sing psalms.
14 Is any sick among you? let him call for the elders of the church; and let them pray over him, anointing him with oil in the name of the Lord:
15 And the prayer of faith shall save the sick, and the Lord shall raise him up; and if he have committed sins, they shall be forgiven him.

16 Confess your faults one to another, and pray one for another, that ye may be healed. The effectual fervent prayer of a righteous man availeth much.

AMP

13 *Is anyone among you afflicted (ill-treated, suffering evil)? He should pray. Is anyone glad at heart? He should sing praise [to God].*

14 *Is anyone among you sick? He should call in the church elders (the spiritual guides). And they should pray over him, anointing him with oil in the Lord's name.*

15 *And the prayer [that is] of faith will save him who is sick, and the Lord will restore him; and if he has committed sins, he will be forgiven.*

16 *Confess to one another therefore your faults (your slips, your false steps, your offenses, your sins) and pray [also] for one another, that you may be healed and restored [to a spiritual tone of mind and heart]. The earnest (heartfelt, continued) prayer of a righteous man makes tremendous power available [dynamic in its working].*

3 JOHN 2

2 Beloved, I wish above all things that thou mayest prosper and be in health, even as thy soul prospereth.

AMP

2 *Beloved, I pray that you may prosper in every way and [that your body] may keep well, even as [I know] your soul keeps well and prospers.*

THE WARFARECOLOGY OF HEALING

THE WARFARECOLOGY OF HEALING
Ephesians 6:10-20

10   Finally, my brethren, be strong in the Lord, and in the power of his might.

11   Put on the whole armour of God, that ye may be able to stand against the wiles of the devil.

12   **For we wrestle not against flesh and blood, but against principalities, against powers, against the rulers of the darkness of this world, against spiritual wickedness in high places.**

13   Wherefore take unto you the whole armour of God, that ye may be able to withstand in the evil day, and having done all, to stand.

14   Stand therefore, having your loins girt about with truth, and having on the breastplate of righteousness;

15   And your feet shod with the preparation of the   gospel of peace;

16   Above all, taking the shield of faith, wherewith ye shall be able to quench all the fiery darts of the wicked.

17   And take the helmet of salvation, and the sword of the Spirit, which is the word of God:

18   Praying always with all prayer and supplication in the Spirit, and watching thereunto with all perseverance and supplication for all saints;

19   And for me, that utterance may be given unto me, that I may open my mouth boldly, to make known the mystery of the gospel,

20 For which I am an ambassador in bonds: that therein I may speak boldly, as I ought to speak.

AMP

10 *In conclusion, be strong in the Lord [be empowered through your union with Him]; draw your strength from Him [that strength which His boundless might provides].*

11 *Put on God's whole armor [the armor of a heavy-armed soldier which God supplies], that you may be able successfully to stand up against [all] the strategies and the deceits of the devil.*

12 ***For we are not wrestling with flesh and blood [contending only with physical opponents], but against the despotisms, against the powers, against [the master spirits who are] the world rulers of this present darkness, against the spirit forces of wickedness in the heavenly (supernatural) sphere.***

13 *Therefore put on God's complete armor, that you may be able to resist and stand your ground on the evil day [of danger], and, having done all [the crisis demands], to stand [firmly in your place].*

14 *Stand therefore [hold your ground], having tightened the belt of truth around your loins and having put on the breastplate of integrity and of moral rectitude and right standing with God,*

15   *And having shod your feet in preparation [to face the enemy with the firm-footed stability, the promptness, and the readiness produced by the good news] of the Gospel of peace.*

16   *Lift up over all the [covering] shield of saving faith, upon which you can quench all the flaming missiles of the wicked [one].*

17   *And take the helmet of salvation and the sword that the Spirit wields, which is the Word of God.*

18   *Pray at all times (on every occasion, in every season) in the Spirit, with all [manner of] prayer and entreaty. To that end keep alert and watch with strong purpose and perseverance, interceding in behalf of all the saints (God's consecrated people).*

19   *And [pray] also for me, that [freedom of] utterance may be given me, that I may open my mouth to proclaim boldly the mystery of the good news (the Gospel),*

20   *For which I am an ambassador in a coupling chain [in prison. Pray] that I may declare it boldly and courageously, as I ought to do.*

Author's Commentary
Ephesians 6:12

It's my firm belief that one of the most destructive reasons why many of us are giving Satan and his demonic forces permission and a right to attack our bodies and minds with sickness and disease is because of **UNFORGIVENESS.**

If we refuse to forgive people and continue to be angry and bitter against them, we give Satan a right (because of the sin of unforgiveness) to consume and attack our body and life.

I strongly encourage you not to wrestle against flesh and blood (people), but to receive the revelation of this verse about who the fight (warfare) is really with and against.

Jesus said if you do not forgive others their trespasses (faults, sins, errors), neither will He forgive your trespasses. Make a choice today to forgive and be healed in Jesus Name! If Jesus has forgiven all our sins, how can we hold any aught against another. Why would we stop your healing and miracle?

Mark 11: 25-26

25 And when ye stand praying, <u>forgive,</u> if ye have ought against any: that your Father also which is in heaven <u>may forgive you</u> your trespasses.

926 **<u>But if ye do not forgive, neither will your Father which is in heaven forgive your trespasses.</u>**

AMP

25 *And whenever you stand praying, if you have anything against anyone, <u>forgive him</u> and let it drop (leave it, let it go), in order that your Father Who is in heaven <u>may also forgive you</u> your [own] failings and shortcomings and let them drop.*

26 ***<u>But if you do not forgive, neither will your Father in heaven forgive your failings and shortcomings.</u>***

Chapter

THE WILL OF GOD FOR YOU!

THE WILL OF GOD FOR YOU!
3 JOHN 1-4

¹The elder unto the well-beloved Gaius, whom I love in the truth.

²Beloved, I wish above all things that thou mayest prosper and be in health, even as thy soul prospereth.

³For I rejoiced greatly, when the brethren came and testified of the truth that is in thee, even as thou walkest in the truth.

⁴I have no greater joy than to hear that my children walk in truth.

AMP

¹*The elderly elder [of the church addresses this letter] to the beloved (esteemed) Gaius, whom I truly love.*

²*Beloved, I pray that you may prosper in every way and [that your body] may keep well, even as [I know] your soul keeps well and prospers.*

³*In fact, I greatly rejoiced when [some of] the brethren from time to time arrived and spoke [so highly] of the sincerity and fidelity of your life, as indeed you do live in the Truth [the whole Gospel presents].*

⁴*I have no greater joy than this, to hear that my [spiritual] children are living their lives in the Truth.*

Author's Commentary
3 John 1-4

It is my second firm belief that there is much confusion whether it is the will and desire of the Lord to heal and work miracles in our lives. As our soul prospers in the Lord, our body which is the temple of the Holy Spirit, the Spirit of God, is to also be well and in good health. Jesus was sent to destroy the works of the devil, which includes sin, sickness, disease, etc. in our lives.

Remember, God so *loved* the world that He gave (gifted us) His only begotten Son, to help and to deliver us from all destructions. Sickness and disease is a destructive work of the kingdom of darkness.

As we believe God for our healing, we must also remember that there are both "natural and spiritual" laws working in our bodies. Many violate the natural laws of the body through poor diet practices, eating habits, and lack of exercise. We must cooperate with the Lord in our pursuit and belief for healing by doing the things we know are right to do, like eating healthy and exercising.

From the spiritual side of our faith for healing, leave every healing prayer line where the preacher says, "If it be thy will Lord; or, If it be the will of the Lord..." Respond to those types of prayers and words like Forrest Gump, and RUN Forrest RUN!

Third John 2 tells us the will of God; and, that's what we pray without wavering. We are to pray, believe, and not faint! Why should we stop our healing and miracle by thinking that the Lord doesn't want His best for us? **Believe and receive!**

> *As we believe God for our healing, we must also remember that there are both "natural and spiritual" laws working in our bodies.*

All law "violations" come with Penalties!

Chapter 5

INGREDIENTS FOR HEALING & MANIFESTATION

CONCLUSION
THE INGREDIENTS OF HEALING

I am persuaded that the disposition and manifestation for your healing is centered in the ingredients of *faith and power in the Word of God* through the Person and Name of our Lord and Savior, Jesus Christ, and the Holy Spirit! The stripes that were placed upon Jesus' back were placed for your healing and victory over every sickness and disease.

1 Peter 2:24

24 Who his own self bare our sins in his own body on the tree, that we, being dead to sins, should live unto righteousness: **by whose stripes ye were healed.**

AMP

24 He personally bore our sins in His (own) body on the tree (as on an altar and offered Himself on it), that we might die (cease to exist) to sin and live to righteousness. ***By His wounds you have been healed.***

The Manifestation
(The Incubation Period)

He *sent* His *word,* and healed them...
Psalm 107:20(a)

While waiting for the manifestation of your healing, please understand the word **Incubation!**

Incubation is the period of time *after* the *word* has been *sent,* <u>enters your body,</u> and <u>begins to work in your body</u> *to produce* what your faith expects; the manifestation of healing when your symptoms no longer appear.

As a born-again Christian, your healing has already been delivered and received through the forgiveness of your sins, as proclaimed in and through the power of God's Word!

As an unbeliever, please know that our God is merciful and gracious. He can heal the unjust as well as the just because He is a good God! It doesn't matter if we are rich or poor, male or female, because God is not a respecter of persons. He responds to *faith in His Word!* It has nothing to do with any assumed goodness on our part. It's all because of the goodness of the Lord that He does what He does.

However, there is a more excellent way of receiving your healing through breaking the curse of sickness and disease. That more excellent way is by asking Jesus Christ, the Son of God, to forgive you of your sins and to come into your heart. Without Christ in our lives, we have no hope.

If you want to receive Christ into your heart, refer to the **General Confession Prayer** on page 11. Your life will never be the same. In Jesus' Name! ∎

Chapter

6

MY
PRAYER
DECREE
FOR YOU!

MY PRAYER DECREE FOR YOU!

I decree and declare that victory, healing, and restoration shall be your portion as you read, proclaim, believe, and receive as truth the scriptures written in this **Word Power Series *for* Healing** book for your life and the lives of those you love.

I declare that this book will be used as a mighty weapon against all the forces of darkness operating in your life and body as it pertains to the perfected will of God proclaimed in the Word of God for you.

I declare and decree that no weapon formed against you shall prosper or bring any fruit of pain and destruction in your life and body. Your body is the temple of the Holy Spirit and nothing defiled shall enter and/or remain.

I declare and decree that sickness and disease is a trespasser in your body and must be evicted from the temple of the Holy Spirit NOW!

I cast out "every" form, shape, seed, or root of sickness from your body and command healing to be sent into your body NOW. Be healed and restored to health NOW. In Jesus' Name. Amen! ∎

++Apostle Kevin E. Kemp, Sr.

A Prayer Decree For You!
(Family or Friend)

I touch and agree in faith with the Prayer Decree of Apostle Kemp over me *(my family or friend)* in Jesus' Name and receive the healing and restoration power of God into my body and life NOW. In the name of Jesus, I am *(they are)* healed. Amen! ∎

Chapter

BOOK READING THOUGHTS, REVELATIONS, AND TESTIMONIES

My Thoughts

My Thoughts

My Thoughts

My Thoughts

Chapter 8

TESTIMONIES & KKM PARTNERSHIP CONTACT INFORMATION

Testimonies and Ministry Partnership

If you have been bless, touched, or healed by the reading and receiving of this book; or would like to become a Kevin Kemp Ministries International "Faith Partner" to help us reach the Nations with the Gospel and Healing power of Jesus Christ, please contact us.

For Faith Partnership, Ministry Donations, Testimonies, Crusade, Conference, Revival, and Seminar Bookings
Contact Information:
Kevin Kemp Ministries (KKM) International Inc.
Attn: Kevin Kemp Media Ministries
Post Office Box 35751
Fayetteville, North Carolina 28303
Office: 919.455.6930
Email: kevinkempministries@gmail.com
Website: www.kevinkempministries.org
Alternate Website: www.BAMInternational.us
For Donations: Click "Donate" link at our Website or via *Paypal* using our Email address

Word Power Series Books
Word Power Series for HEALING!
Word Power Series for DELIVERANCE!
Word Power Series for THE BLESSING!
Word Power Series for FAITH!

Thank You!

for supporting our
International Television and
World Outreach Ministries

PRAYERFULLY CONSIDER
becoming a
Kevin Kemp Ministries
International
"FAITH PARTNER"
TODAY!